MARK TWAIN

AND HUCKLEBERRY FINN

BY STEWART ROSS

illustrated by

RONALD HIMLER

VIKING

VIKING
Published by the Penguin Group
Penguin Putnam Books for Young Readers, 345 Hudson Street, New York, New York 10014, U.S.A.
Penguin Books Ltd, 27 Wrights Lane, London W8 5TZ, England
Penguin Books Australia Ltd, Ringwood, Victoria, Australia
Penguin Books Canada Ltd, 10 Alcorn Avenue, Toronto, Ontario, Canada M4V 3B2
Penguin Books (N.Z.) Ltd, 182-190 Wairau Road, Auckland 10, New Zealand

Penguin Books Ltd, Registered Offices: Harmondsworth, Middlesex, England

First published in 1999 by Viking, a member of Penguin Putnam Books for Young Readers

1 3 5 7 9 10 8 6 4 2

LIBRARY OF CONGRESS CATALOGING-IN-PUBLICATION DATA
Ross, Stewart.
Mark Twain and Huckleberry Finn / by Stewart Ross; illustrated by Ronald Himler.
p. cm.
Summary: Examines the personal life and literary career of the American author of many well-known books,
including the somewhat controversial title, "The Adventures of Huckleberry Finn."
ISBN 0-670-88181-3
1. Twain, Mark 1835-1910—Juvenile literature. 2. Twain, Mark, 1835–1910. Adventures of Huckleberry Finn—Juvenile literature.
3. Literature and society—United States—History—19th century—Juvenile literature.
4. Adventure stories, American—History and criticism—Juvenile literature. 5. Authors, American—19th century—Biography—
Juvenile literature. 6. Finn, Huckleberry (Fictitious character)—Juvenile literature. 7. Boys in literature—Juvenile literature.
[1. Twain, Mark, 1835–1910. 2. Authors, American. 3. Twain, Mark, 1835–1910. Adventures of Huckleberry Finn.]
I. Himler, Ronald, ill. II. Title.
PS1331.R66 1999 813'.4—dc21 98-29892 CIP AC

Manufactured in Hong Kong. Set in New Baskerville
Book design by Eileen Rosenthal

To all young people who refuse to be "sivilized."
—S. R.

HANNIBAL

The preacher placed his hands on the edge of the pulpit and leaned heavily forward. "Brothers and sisters of Hannibal," he began, "hear ye the word of the Lord."

Sitting bolt upright in the front pew, Judge John Clemens lifted his face toward the preacher. Beside him his wife Jane, with Henry Clemens on her knee, gazed modestly down at her prayer book. The two oldest children, Orion and Pamela, waited seriously for the preacher to continue. On the end of the row, young Sam yawned.

"My message," thundered the preacher, "comes from the Book of Books. In his mercy the Good Lord has given it us, that we shall be saved." He paused to let his words sink in. The interior of the Old Ship of Zion Methodist Church was as still as stone.

Out on the river, a stern-wheeler hooted. The preacher glared down at his congregation, as if daring them to react to the sound. "Hear the words of Saint Paul in his letter to the Christians of Rome," he roared. "Chapter six, verse twenty-three. Hear them, brothers and sisters, and bind them close to your hearts."

Sam Clemens leaned towards his sister Pamela. "'The wages of sin is death,' I bet," he whispered. Pamela ignored him.

"These words, O children of Hannibal, are your salvation," went on the preacher. "'The wages of sin is death!'"

"I was right!" Sam said, grinning. His father looked across at him and frowned. Trust Sam, he thought, not to take things seriously.

✣ ✣ ✣

In the 1840s there was an uncertain frontier feel about the town of Hannibal, Missouri. Settlers and steamboats, traders and crooks arrived, hung around a while, then moved on. Only two things never changed: the rolling flood of the Mississippi and the honesty of Judge Clemens.

John Marshall Clemens was not a great man, although he was said to be descended from a judge who had condemned King Charles I to death. The justice of the peace was certainly not a rich man, either. His legal fees were low and he worked as a clerk to make up his income. He failed as a trader, storekeeper, and land speculator. His 100,000 acres in Tennessee, bought for a mere five hundred dollars, never yielded the expected fortune. At times his family lived in a home that was little more than a two-room log house.

Whatever his business weaknesses, Virginia-born John Clemens was not called "Judge" for nothing. He was unfailingly honest and respectable. Despite his lack of cash, he saw that his children were properly brought up. They always wore shoes—in the winter, at least. He owned three slaves, was chairman of the Library Committee, and served on the Roads Committee. In the fall of 1845, to improve himself, he took English grammar lessons. Judge Clemens was a pillar of the community.

Mrs. Clemens, born Jane Lampton in Kentucky, was an ideal partner for her dry, upright husband. She, too, was rumored to have noble ancestors— the British Earls of Durham—and in later life Sam sometimes made joking remarks about his famous forebears. As was usual for middle-class women of her time, she did not go out to work. Instead, she devoted herself to the welfare of her husband and children.

Jane seems to have been a warm-hearted and friendly woman. If we believe Sam (not always a wise thing to do), she was a firm friend of the oppressed, both man and beast. Once, seeing a young girl running down the street to avoid a beating from her father, she sheltered the child and told the man she would thrash him if he laid a finger on his daughter. On another occasion she snatched the whip from the hand of rider who was cruelly flogging his horse. Learning from his mother's example, Sam too developed a genuine sympathy for the underdog. It was not always appreciated. Years later, when working in San Francisco, he was imprisoned for making blunt comments about the brutality of the city police department.

Two of the Clemenses' children, Margaret and Benjamin, died young. Orion, like his father, was full of schemes that he believed would one day make his fortune but never did. The musically gifted Pamela gave piano and guitar lessons to help the family finances. The youngest child, Henry, was the darling of the family. Sam said he could not remember him ever doing a vicious thing, and probably used him as a starting point for the character of Sid Sawyer in *The Adventures of Tom Sawyer*.

Sam was two years older than Henry. Born Samuel Langhorne Clemens in Florida, Missouri, on November 30, 1835, he was four when his family moved to Hannibal. Weak and sickly during his early years, he was toughened by a vigorous, open-air boyhood on the river and in the Missouri countryside. He remained lean all his life, with narrow shoulders and a head slightly too large for his body. By his late teens he had matured into a strong young man of middle height with attractive, wavy hair. He told anyone willing to listen that he was very good-looking.

✣   ✣   ✣

Sam Clemens had two childhoods. The first—formal and annoying—was his shoes-on existence. It meant behaving as a son of the Judge ought to behave. He crawled unwillingly to Dawson's schoolhouse, where he was bored and badly behaved. In the Methodist Church he fidgeted through endless services and became a lifelong unbeliever. For a short time, aged fifteen, he paraded with the anti-tobacco Cadets of Temperance. The strain was too great. He left the group, smoked what he said in his *Autobiography* was "the best cigar that was ever made," and remained a lifelong heavy smoker.

Sam's shoes-off childhood began where the first ended, outside Hannibal's sleepy and often corrupt slave-owning society. It revolved around the broad Mississippi river, Glasscock's Island, the old mill, open countryside, and mysterious McDowell's Cave. The personalities that burned themselves into the young lad's memory were not the worthy citizens of Hannibal, but its colorful rogues and outsiders.

There was Jimmy Finn, the town drunkard. When Judge Clemens tried to dry him out, he met with his usual lack of success. There was "Uncle Dan'l," the kindly middle-aged slave of Sam's uncle, John A. Quarles. When it came to storytelling, no one could match the silver-tongued Uncle Dan'l. The long summers spent on John and Patsy Quarles's farm were among the boy's fondest memories. The couple believed that all folk, good and bad, would enter the Kingdom of Heaven, and they were unfailingly kind to Sam and everyone else they met.

The Blankenship family, on the other hand, were not kind. They were not mean either—not in the traditional sense, anyway. They had drifted into Hannibal from South Carolina and lived in a ramshackle barn of a house in Hill Street. The parents drank. The children went neither to school nor to church. According to the town gossips, the daughters hung about getting up to no good. The boys were left to their own devices. Two of them exercised a magical charm over the young Sam, particularly because the Judge's children were forbidden to associate with such rough, heathen types.

Benson Blankenship—"Bunce" to his friends—made a living by fishing. His younger brother Tom did nothing in particular. Barefoot and tattered, the young urchin passed his days hunting rabbits, exploring, scrounging, and scavenging for food—doing his best to keep out of the way of civilization. He was tough, sharp, and ignorant. But as Sam saw only too clearly, Tom was also cheerful, good-hearted, and above all, free.

The older Sam grew, the more fond his memories became of the ill-fed lad who led their childhood games and laughed at the "Miss Nancy" softness of his well-brought-up playmates. By middle age Sam yearned for the innocence and freedom of "the only really independent person—boy or man—in the community." It was an impossible dream. But it was also a fertile one, and it inspired Sam's finest creation: Huckleberry Finn.

Three incidents stuck like flies in the web of Sam's memory. On January 24, 1845, in Hannibal's first premeditated murder, the merchant William

Owsley shot "Uncle Sam" Smarr. Uncle Sam was not a bad fellow, but after a few drinks his tongue grew a bit rough. Claiming he had been provoked, Owsley was found not guilty. Sam was stirred by the blatant injustice. He could do nothing about it at the time. Later, however, in Colonel Sherburn's cruel shooting of old Boggs in *The Adventures of Huckleberry Finn*, he made his feelings of outrage quite clear.

About this time a couple of English actors passed through town and staged a ridiculous sword fight from Shakespeare's *Richard III*. Sam was too young to understand much of what went on. But in *Huckleberry Finn*, written after he had come to appreciate the supreme master of the English language, he mocks those who mangle Shakespeare for profit and scorns the ignorant folk who support their talentless shows.

More seriously, in 1847 Bunce made friends with an escaped slave hiding on Sny Island near the Illinois shore. Ignoring the reward for the man's recapture, Bunce took him food for several weeks before the fugitive was discovered by woodcutters and chased into a swamp. A few days later Sam and a few friends crossed to Sny Island for a bit of fishing and nutting. As they were poking about in the mire, the mutilated body of the runaway slave rose grimly to the surface.

Sam did not forget the ghastly image, or the cruel circumstances that had created it.

✤ ✤ ✤

Sam was the hope of the family. He was intelligent and had no problems with schoolwork—when he set his mind to it. But he was not an easy child. He walked in his sleep, rarely did as he was told, and swung swiftly between rage and remorse. Adventure was his great love. In his vivid imagination the real and the fictional often overlapped—he claimed he had been saved from drowning nine times before learning to swim.

There was nothing made up about the next major event in Sam's life. In March 1847, when Sam was eleven, Judge Clemens died of pneumonia. Some sixty years later Sam remembered, or thought he remembered, standing before his father's open casket and begging his mother to be allowed to leave school.

"No, Sammy," replied his mother, "you need not go to school anymore. Only promise to be a better boy. Promise not to break my heart."

"FORTY TO FIFTY YEARS AGO"

The title page of *The Adventures of Huckleberry Finn* read, "SCENE: THE MISSISSIPPI VALLEY" and "TIME: FORTY TO FIFTY YEARS AGO." The U.S.A. was then, in the 1830s, about sixty years old, and the U.S. government controlled vast territories where land was sold at knock-down prices. This was how John Clemens had got his acres in Tennessee.

The population was growing at an extraordinary 35 percent per decade, bringing new wealth and opportunities. By 1820, the U.S. had become the world's leading cotton producer, and the output of other agricultural produce was soaring. By 1860, one thousand steam-powered stern-wheelers plied the Mississippi, turning it into a highway that linked the heart of the country to the sea. They put Hannibal on the map.

Slavery was entrenched in the South. "In my schooldays," Sam said in his *Autobiography*, "slavery was as much a fact of life as church going." Slave owning was a mark of status: John Clemens's three slaves raised him above his run-of-the-mill white neighbors.

Early in the century a Christian revival swept the country, inspiring reform movements such as the campaign for the abolition of slavery. If we believe Sam Clemens, around Hannibal religious enthusiasm usually meant ranting and bigotry. At the same time, a grass-roots, distinctly American culture was appearing in songs, minstrel shows, story-telling, newspaper stories, and public lectures. It could be vigorous, colloquial, and very funny. As yet, however, it had not found a voice powerful enough to carry it into the homes of the folk Huck Finn called "sivilized." Bridging this gap would be Sam Clemens's outstanding achievement.

MARK TWAIN

Sam made a dull start to his career with words. After Judge Clemens's death, Joseph P. Ament hired Sam as an apprentice printer on the *Hannibal Courier*. Instead of wages, he received full board and his boss's cast-off clothing. The shirts enveloped him like circus tents.

Two years later Orion Clemens established a rival paper in Hannibal, the *Western Union*. Sam, promised a decent living, left Ament to work for his brother. However, there was something in all the Clemenses that guaranteed business failure, and Orion was no exception. Sam got no wages, and in May 1853, the paper failed. Aged seventeen, he went off to St. Louis to work as a typesetter on the *Evening News*.

For three years he traveled about the East and Midwest, scraping a living as a printer and subeditor. To his passion for tobacco, which he passed on to Huckleberry Finn, he added a liking for strong drink. He was fascinated by everyone he met—particularly the crooks—and closely observed every detail of their looks, speech, and behavior. His feeling for language was fed by wide reading and a keen ear for dialect.

Despite his many experiences and adventures, Sam still had no idea what he wanted to do with his life. His thirst for adventure was not quenched, but he wanted more than just thrills. For a time he even considered becoming a preacher. To the insecure and often lonely and depressed young man, a preacher's life would have brought the attention, affection, and wealth he yearned for. But he dropped the idea when he realized he did not have what he called "the necessary stock in trade—i.e. religion."

✣ ✣ ✣

The first sign that Sam might be famous one day came in 1852. In May the humorous Boston magazine *Carpet Bag* featured his first printed short story, "The Dandy Frightening the Squatter." This success did not make choosing a career any easier. Although writing came easily to him, he did not yet think it a realistic pathway to riches and fame.

By 1855 Sam was back with Orion, working for him as a printer in Keokuk, Iowa. Once again, he was paid very little. He wrote a bit, continued to read, watched the world around him—and dreamed. To his delight, that November one of his dreams came true. He found a fifty-dollar bill in the street. He had never seen so much money before. When no one claimed it, he went to Cincinnati as the first step on a journey to the upper reaches of the Amazon. Inspired by the reports of explorers, he planned to make his fortune trading in cocaine. (At that time, doctors used the drug, which was legal, as an anesthetic.)

A man named Horace Bixby kept Sam Clemens on American soil. Or rather, on American waters. Bixby piloted the stern-wheeler on which Sam traveled downriver to New Orleans. The two got chatting, and Sam was sometimes allowed to take the wheel. He was enchanted. By the time he reached the sea, he had forgotten all about Brazil and cocaine. He was going to train with Bixby as a Mississippi pilot.

The apprenticeship cost Sam five hundred dollars. He borrowed one hundred dollars from his sister Pamela's husband, William A. Moffett, and promised to pay the rest when he was earning. His years on the river were among the best of his life. "A pilot in those days," he wrote twenty-five years later in *Life on the Mississippi*, "was the only unfettered and entirely independent being that lived on the earth." A single tragedy marred this blissful existence. In the spring of 1858, the engines of the stern-wheeler *Pennsylvania*, on which Sam's kindly younger brother Henry was working,

blew up. Henry was thrown clear but swam back to the wreck to help with the rescue. A jet of steam entered his lungs, and he died in great agony. Sam, who had recently urged his brother always to put others first, blamed himself for Henry's death.

Sam received his pilot's license in April 1859. He worked for two years, until the Civil War put an end to river traffic and he had to find new employment. Wandering back to Hannibal, he joined a band of Confederate irregulars known as the Marion Rangers. After two weeks of rain and retreat, he deserted. Whatever else he might be, Sam Clemens was not a soldier.

✤ ✤ ✤

Once more, Sam drifted. He went out west to the Nevada Territory, where Orion had been appointed Secretary to the territory as a reward for helping Abraham Lincoln get elected. After wasting his energies as a prospector and a timber speculator, Sam fell back on the one job he knew he could handle without difficulty. In August 1862 he joined the *Virginia City Territorial Enterprise* as a full-time reporter and feature writer. Before long he had become a popular journalist. He did not claim to write great literature in the traditional style. His talent was for using ordinary language to capture the mood of everyday America and make his readers laugh.

Sam Clemens had finally found his vocation. As if to celebrate the fact, he changed his name. On February 2, 1863, he wrote his first piece under the pseudonym "Mark Twain." In future years he would say this was the cry of a stern-wheeler deckhand calling out the depth. "Mark twain!" was two fathoms or twelve feet. Sam claimed he took the name from Captain Isaiah Sellers, who had used it as a pen name in the 1850s. Since then others have suggested a less poetic origin for the phrase. "Mark twain!" was also Sam's cry to the bartender to mark up two drinks on his tab!

The talent of the nearly thirty-year-old Sam Clemens did not go unnoticed. Among his admirers were Bret Harte, the successful writer and editor of *The Californian*, and the humorist and lecturer Artemus Ward. Sam studied Ward closely, learning from him how to woo and capture an audience. Success did not make Sam content, however. He swung between idleness and surges of fanatical energy. One minute he was bursting with enthusiasm, the next he was in deep despair. In 1866 he even thought about taking his own life. He was capable of flaring fury, too, followed by pitiful remorse. After only two years on the *Territorial Enterprise* he challenged another editor to a duel and had to flee to California.

✢ ✢ ✢

While working for the *San Francisco Morning Call*, Sam made his major breakthrough. In November 1865 his story "The Celebrated Jumping Frog of Calaveras County" was printed by *The Saturday Press* of New York. Readers loved the tale, and it was widely reprinted elsewhere. On the strength of a single story, his name became known throughout America.

At last, Sam Clemens was a man with a future.

FAIRYLAND

Success bred success. In 1866 the Sacramento *Union* paid Sam to visit Honolulu in the Sandwich Islands (now Hawaii) and send his impressions back to the paper. He reckoned his writing had made him "about the best-known honest man on the Pacific coast." Eager to cash in on his fame, he made his debut as a speaker, lecturing on his experiences overseas. "Admission one dollar," read the advertisement. "Doors open at half past seven, the trouble begins at 8 o'clock." Sam was always great at publicizing his own work. The talk was a spectacular hit. From this time onward his dry, naive delivery, dandy appearance, and exaggerated Southern drawl never failed to charm audiences the world over. Before long he had become one of the finest comic speakers of the century.

At the end of the year Sam was off again. He was offered twenty dollars a week by the *Alta California* to send letters back from New York. The handsome wage allowed him to support his mother, his luckless brother Orion, and his sister Pamela, now a widow. Sam found the city a lonely place. But between his usual bouts of drinking, brawling, and depression he lectured and wrote with increasing confidence. He also enjoyed the publication of his first book. *The Celebrated Jumping Frog of Calaveras County, and Other Sketches* appeared in April 1867, neatly printed with a golden frog on the front. Although well received, it sold few copies. Sam was plagued with depression and self-doubt. He needed a change.

✢ ✢ ✢

On June 8, the *Quaker City* sailed from New York for a long cruise of the Mediterranean and the Holy Land. On board were the crew, some seventy-five passengers (mostly middle-aged and pious) and the famous humorist Mark Twain. He had been commissioned to send reports back to the *Alta California* and *New York Tribune*. Commentator and pilgrims could not have been more different. He found the voyage out "a funeral without a corpse," a dull round of "solemnity, decorum, dinner, dominoes, prayers, slander." To most of his fellow passengers he was a sharp and ungodly drunkard. He was not impressed by the palace of Versailles and even less by Palestine. The cost of hiring a boat on the Sea of Galilee was so high, he quipped, that he was not surprised Christ had chosen to walk on the water. The high point of his cruise was when fellow passenger Charley Langdon showed him an ivory miniature of his twenty-one-year-old sister Olivia. Sam claimed to be in love with her from that moment for the rest of his life.

However much he disliked his transatlantic jaunt, Sam made the most of it. In November 1867 Elisha Bliss of the American Publishing Company, Hartford, suggested he publish his observations in book form. Early in the new year Sam traveled to Hartford, Connecticut, to hammer out the contract. The sophistication of Hartford and the beauty of the surrounding country-side made a deep impression on him. He remembered particularly seeing children gathering wild huckleberries. Contracted to provide a 240,000-word manuscript for Bliss to publish by subscription, by early summer 1868 he was beavering away at his task.

Meanwhile, Sam had caught up again with Charley Langdon. In December, when the Langdons were in New York, he met Olivia for the first time. He made a good enough impression to be invited to visit the Langdons at their home in Elmira, New York. Sam found the real Olivia—or "Livy" as she was known in the family—every bit as charming as her ivory miniature.

Ten years younger than Sam, Livy was an innocent and affectionate hypochondriac. She was also a devout Christian and disapproved of Sam's wayward habits. In short, she was everything he was not. But opposite poles attract. She found him amusing and interesting. He saw in her all he had dreamed of in a woman—beauty, warmth, and great kindliness. His feelings were no doubt helped by the fact that she came from a wealthy and respected family of East Coast gentry. Jervis Langdon, Livy's father, was a broad-minded businessman who had made his fortune from the coal and iron industry.

Sam completed his cruise book, *The Innocents Abroad*, during the early summer. He had it read by Bret Harte and handed it over to Bliss in August. Three months later Livy agreed to marry him, but insisted on keeping their engagement secret for the moment. Overjoyed, Sam took himself off on his first major lecture tour, speaking on "The American Vandal Abroad."

Before the Langdons would consent to his daughter's marriage, they asked Sam to provide references for his good character. He gave a list of people they could write to, but included no close friends. There was no point in asking them, he said later, because he knew they would lie for him. The replies were hardly flattering. "Clemens is a humbug," said one. He "would fill a drunkard's grave," predicted another. Startled, Jervis Langdon asked Sam whether he had any friends at all. "Apparently not," came the reply. Langdon liked the man's honesty and said he would be his friend. As a result, in February 1869, Sam Clemens and Livy Langdon were formally engaged to be married.

The businessman's faith seemed to have been justified when *The Innocents Abroad* was published in July. It was an immediate success. Moreover, unusually for a book published by subscription, it was well reviewed by serious literary magazines. William Dean Howells, writing in Boston's weighty *Atlantic Monthly*, said that among humorists Mark Twain was now "quite worthy of the company of the best."

Jervis Langdon showed his approval of his future son-in-law by lending him $25,000 to buy a share in the *Buffalo Express*. A still more generous gesture followed. On the day after his marriage to Livy—February 2, 1870—Jervis presented Sam with a box. Inside were a large check and the deeds to a "fairy palace"—a furnished mansion in Buffalo worth $43,000.

Sam Clemens had arrived.

"ANOTHER BOYS' BOOK"

"The secret source of humor itself," Sam said towards the end of his life, "is not joy but sorrow." Beneath his wit and sparkle, his showing off and public good humor, the true Sam Clemens was never happy for long. Even the joys of domestic bliss and prosperity were short-lived.

He did little work in 1870, although he was contracted to write a book about Nevada and California (*Roughing It*). His time was taken up first with his marriage, then with the death of his father-in-law, which brought the pregnant Livy to the point of collapse, and finally with the birth of a son in November. Langdon Clemens was a premature, sickly baby. Family illnesses and the financial pressure of living beyond his means brought Sam close to despair. The more depressed he became, the more difficult he was to live with.

Eighteen-seventy-one was another tough year. To raise money, he sold the family home and his share in the *Buffalo Express* (both for less than they were worth) and went back to lecturing. He spent the summer with his family at Quarry Farm, Livy's sister's country house in the hills above Elmira. Only here did he find the peace he needed to write. In the fall the Clemenses rented a house in Hartford, the town that had so impressed Sam when he had first visited it three years previously. He was delighted to have some of America's leading publishers and writers as neighbors, but still had to retire to the hills to do any serious work.

Over the next two years Sam's fortunes steadily recovered. *Roughing It*, published in February 1872, sold well. Later in the year he crossed the Atlantic. He was planning to write about the corruption of the Old World. He found England so pleasant, however, that he abandoned his original idea. Instead, he cooperated with his neighbor Charles Dudley Warner to write *The Gilded Age*, an attack on American corruption. With his usual disregard for the truth, he claimed that *he* put the facts into the book, while Warner added the fiction. The summer of 1874 saw him in full flow once more. He worked on *Tom Sawyer*, successfully adapted *The Gilded Age* for the stage, and wrote regularly for the *Atlantic Monthly*.

Sam was a rich man again. Always the showman, he needed to display his wealth to the world. The result was 351 Farmington Avenue, Hartford, a nineteen-room mansion built and furnished to his own eccentric design at a cost of $122,000. It was enlarged in 1881. The way Livy managed the household further increased his admiration for her. He seemed to picture her, as he would the young women in *Huckleberry Finn*, as some sort of goddess living above the sordid world of men. Despite Livy's careful housekeeping, however, the costs of the new establishment were gigantic. The more Sam earned, the more he spent. It was a recipe for great strain, if not disaster.

There were four in the Clemens family when they moved into the new house in the fall of 1874. Olivia Susan, known as Susy, was two and Clara only a few months old. A fourth child, Jean, was born in July 1880. Some years later she was found to suffer from epilepsy. The sickly Langdon had died of diphtheria three months after Susy's birth. Sam believed he had brought on his son's death by allowing him to catch cold. Remembering the fate of his brother Henry, he gloomily insisted that he now had the deaths of two of his family on his conscience. Guilt and self-pity fed his bouts of depression.

✤ ✤ ✤

Nearing his fortieth birthday, with money in his pocket and time on his hands, Sam was drawn toward the world he had left. A huge gulf separated the Sam Clemens of Hartford from the Sam Clemens of Hannibal, and he looked back on his boyhood with a mixture of love and contempt. He had

Bret Harte

Artemus Ward

William Dean
Howells

"THE GILDED AGE"

After the Civil War, America was more aggressive and dynamic than ever before. Sam was thrilled and horrified by what was happening. The country's new technology and wealth amazed him. But he was afraid that beneath its gilded surface the U.S. was losing its soul.

"Money-lust," he wrote, was making the country "hard, sordid, ungentle, dishonest, oppressive." Child labor was widespread. President Grant's administration (1869–77), which Mark Twain and Charles Dudley Warner satirized in *The Gilded Age* (1873), was poisoned by corrupt politicians. The defeated South was becoming a backwater of racial cruelty, where four and a half million black Americans were still virtually enslaved by low pay and prejudice. Along the banks of the Mississippi, Sam's beloved stern-wheelers rotted in the sunshine.

New schools, colleges, libraries, newspapers, and magazines were springing up in every state. Americans developed a huge appetite for books, many sold by subscription publishing, in which salespeople showed half-educated families what the books would look like and got them to pay in advance. Critics disliked the system because it emphasized appearance above content. This made their praise for Twain's *The Innocents Abroad*, all the more remarkable.

A fresh and original style of American writing was emerging. Its writers were not interested in sentimentality and "grand" prose but in everyday experiences, language, and humor. Leaders of the movement included Artemus Ward and William Dean Howells. So when Howells reviewed *The Innocents Abroad* favorably, he knew what he was about. He immediately recognized Twain as a writer of real power—the true voice of America.

lived out the American dream—log cabin to mansion. Yet he could not have achieved one without the other. He had succeeded in spite of—and because of—his drawling speech, homespun directness, and backwoods humor. They were his unique appeal.

Tragically, the contrast between who Sam was and where he had come from split him in "Twain." He was two people who could never meet: Mark Twain the rebel and Sam Clemens would-be socialite. One despised high society, the other cried out to be accepted by it. With remarkable insight, Livy often referred to him affectionately as her "Little Man"—the boy from Missouri who never grew up. And like a child, Sam was becoming still more moody, and sometimes violent. He once threw all his shirts out of the bathroom window because a single button was missing.

✢ ✢ ✢

Sam's first voyage back to pre-war Missouri was the novel *Tom Sawyer*. He started it one summer, set it aside, and finished it the next. The story of a young boy's adventures in small-town Missouri before the Civil War had no plan but was allowed to "follow its own drift." When he finished, Sam reckoned he had written a book for adults. A few months later he changed his mind and declared *Tom Sawyer* to be "a book for boys, pure and simple." Published in 1876, it sold only 24,000 copies in the first year. A Canadian publisher had flooded the market with a pirated version before the real one appeared. Sam was furious but undaunted.

The writing of *Tom Sawyer* was followed by a series for the *Atlantic Monthly* entitled "Old Times on the Mississippi." The subject still haunted him, and during the fall of 1875 an idea for a new novel was beginning to form in his mind. By the summer of 1876, "more to be at work than anything else," he was back in his specially built octagonal summer house at Quarry Farm, "tearing along" on what he first called "another boys' book."

✢ ✢ ✢

When in this sort of humor, Sam worked very fast. He could write up to four thousand words (more than ten pages of a book) each day, letting

leaves of manuscript flutter to the floor as he completed them. Plot was of little interest to him. A story evolved like a journey down an unknown river—he had no idea what lay round the next bend, but knew he would eventually get to the end. If the language, characters, and incidents were right, the story that held them together would look after itself. Aware of the problems this could bring, he wrote at the start of his manuscript: "Persons attempting to find a motive in this narrative will be prosecuted; persons attempting to find a moral in it will be banished; persons attempting to find a plot in it will be shot." Like much else he wrote, the comment should not be taken too seriously.

Sam soon realized that he was writing more than what he had called "a kind of companion to *Tom Sawyer.*" It was a work of greater depth. Using a framework of short episodes, he examined how "a sound heart and a deformed conscience come into collision and conscience suffers defeat." This idea, that true and honest instincts are in danger of being crushed by education, sums up his view of American society and human nature in general. The book's wit did not make it any less serious. The purpose of humor, he once wrote, was the "deriding of shams, the exposure of pretentious falsities, the laughing of stupid superstitions out of existence." It was the "natural friend of human rights and human liberties."

Although Sam liked what he had written, by December his inspiration had withered. He set the manuscript aside, having written most of chapters one through fourteen. For the next three years he was plagued with more financial worries, quarrels with other writers and publishers, and concern for Livy's health. A second stage play was an expensive flop. Sam considered setting up his own publishing company, worked occasionally on *The Prince and the Pauper*, and in April 1878 took his family to Europe.

The European experience gave Sam material for another success, *A Tramp Abroad*. Meanwhile, in 1879–80 he picked up *Huck Finn* and completed a few more chapters.

Although he wrote his first drafts rapidly, he rarely let them go to the printers without careful revision. "The difference between the right word and the almost right word is the difference between lightning and the lightning

bug," he declared. The long sentence he hated as "a serpent, with half its arches under the water." He got others to read his work, too. Those he trusted most were Livy and his old friend Howells. Susy Clemens remembers her mother reading Sam's manuscripts to their children, "expurgating" with a pencil the bits she felt were too "strong." To tease her and delight the girls, Sam sometimes put in "delightfully dreadful" passages he did not intend to include in the finished work. In the end, though, Sam always had the final say.

❖ ❖ ❖

By the early 1880s Sam's financial ship had righted itself once more. Livy's health had recovered. He had made his nephew Charles L. Webster his business manager and was sending Orion seventy-five dollars a month. Certain *The Prince and the Pauper* would do well, he put up the money for its publication himself and paid the publisher a royalty. The extraordinary scheme was one of

Sam's few successful business ventures and made him a lot of money.

In the spring of 1882 Sam went to the Mississippi to gather material for the second half of his *Life on the Mississippi*. Little was as he remembered it. The South, he wrote, was "old and bowed and melancholy now." When he visited Hannibal, his eyes filled with tears. Apart from a riotous time in New Orleans with his old river mates, when he said he was "nearer to heaven than I shall ever hope to be again," the trip was bitterly disappointing. Nevertheless, he returned with plenty of notes and ideas for both his Mississippi book and his still unfinished novel.

Safely tucked away in Quarry Farm, in the summer of 1883 Sam finally finished *Huckleberry Finn*. The last chapters simply fell from his pen. "I haven't had such booming working-days for many years," he reported. "This summer it is no more trouble to me to write than it is to lie." Lying was clearly on his mind and became a major theme of the book. The manuscript was revised several times, typed out, and revised again. By the fall of 1884 it was ready for publication.

Life on the Mississippi had appeared in the summer of 1883. It had not sold well, and Sam had returned to lecturing to make ends meet. He blamed the publisher for the book's poor reception. To give *Huckleberry Finn* a better chance, in the winter of 1884 he set up Charles L. Webster Publishing Co. with his nephew in charge. The business got off to a bad start. The British edition of *Huckleberry Finn* appeared in time for Christmas, but the U.S. edition was delayed into the new year. An engraver had added an obscene detail to one of the illustrations, and it had to be reprinted.

The Adventures of Huckleberry Finn was finally published in America on February 18, 1885. Despite the setback, Sam was optimistic. He felt in his bones that he had written a "rattling good" book. "There is not going to be any reason whatever why this book should not succeed," he told Webster, "and it shall and must."

HUCKLEBERRY FINN

"You don't know about me without you have read a book by the name of *The Adventures of Tom Sawyer*," says the boy Huckleberry Finn, "but that ain't no matter." He is quite right. *Huckleberry Finn* is a more adult work, and its central character (inspired by the author's childhood playmate, Tom Blankenship) is far more interesting and complex than Tom Sawyer.

The tale begins in St. Petersburg. The narrow-minded, slave-owning town beside the Mississippi in pre-war Missouri is based on the Hannibal of Mark Twain's (Sam Clemens's) childhood. To escape the "sivilizing" of Widow Douglas, who has taken him in, Huck joins the gang of Tom Sawyer, who has read so many adventure stories that he can't tell playing from real life. In a cave (based on McDowell's cave near Hannibal) they melodramatically sign an oath with their blood. Huck goes along with this and other games because he likes Tom, but he mistrusts his "lies." Tom is not alone in twisting the truth. "I never seen anybody but lied," Huck reflects sadly. The voice of his creator is loud and clear.

The boys meet Jim, a middle-aged slave, whom they call a "nigger." Nowadays this is an extremely offensive word. In the context of the book, however, a different one would have been unrealistic, even dishonest. It was commonly used at the time, and not meant as an insult. Twain is painting a true picture of life in the old South. It is not a pretty sight. Nevertheless, had he been less accurate his criticisms would have lost their bite.

Huck, who came into six thousand dollars at the end of *Tom Sawyer*, is rich. But like the author himself, he is uneasy about the ties money brings. Huck feels "all cramped up" by the widow's attempt to make him a God-fearing, respectable boy. He is also haunted by memories of his drunken, bullying father. Soon after he has given his fortune to the local judge for safekeeping, Pap Finn (modelled on Hannibal's town drunkard, Jimmy Finn) turns up.

Huck flees from his father and has amazing adventures on a raft journey down the Mississippi in the company of Jim, who has run away. On the surface the stories are light-hearted and ironic. The messages they carry, however, are deeply serious. The farcical Shakespearean acting of a pair of con men ("the Duke of Bridgewater" and "the King of France") mocks literary snobbishness. On one occasion Huck is sheltered by the Grangerfords, who have a pointless feud with the neighboring Shepherdsons. After praising a sermon "all about brotherly love, and such-like tiresomeness," the two families start killing each other. Huck is horrified by the tragic slaughter.

Huck's journey is really an education, a series of lessons on the true nature of people and society. His course is littered with bullies, narrow-minded racists, cheats, and vicious criminals. He gradually realizes they are not necessarily bad in themselves but have been made wicked by a dishonest civilization. This dishonesty is Twain's chief target. He names a wrecked steamer after the British romantic novelist Sir Walter Scott, for example, because he believes romantic fiction is a wreck—a backward-looking hodgepodge of quaint myths and brainless shams.

The character of Jim is drawn from "Uncle Dan'l," whom the author had met at the Quarles's farm. His relationship with Huck is the heart of the book. Alone on the raft, beyond the world's prejudices and cruelties, Jim and Huck—black and white—are free and equal. Nevertheless, Huck takes time to overcome his racist upbringing. Only after Jim has been recaptured does Huck see that he must stand by his friend, even if it means breaking the law. He fears he will go to hell for doing this. Twain means, of course, that Huck will go to heaven for making the moral rather than the "sivilized" choice.

"RUNNING DRY"

Not everyone liked *Huckleberry Finn*. Some found it coarse and crude. The Library Committee of Concord, Massachusetts, even banned it from their shelves. Nevertheless, perhaps helped by its vulgar reputation, sales rocketed—51,000 copies by the end of May 1885.

After the five most productive years of his life, Sam was as rich and contented as he would ever be. "It seems that whatever I touch turns to gold," he gloated. It was an ominous remark. His long, sad downhill slide was about to begin. Although only fifty, he would never again reach the creative heights of *Huckleberry Finn*. His attempts to cash in on the fashion for detective stories—*Tom Sawyer Abroad* and *Tom Sawyer, Detective*—were feeble failures. The dark pessimism that had lurked behind *Huckleberry Finn* comes out into the open in *A Connecticut Yankee in King Arthur's Court*. The wacky Twain comedy of the early pages is drowned in a holocaust of slaughter at the end. On finishing the book, Sam said in his *Autobiography*, he was "written out." The "tank" of his inspiration had "run dry."

Only in parts of *Following the Equator*, *The Tragedy of Pudd'nhead Wilson*, and one or two short stories—notably "The Man That Corrupted Hadleyburg" did Sam's old sparkle return. Even then, it was marked with deep cynicism. "Man is the only animal that blushes. Or needs to," he observed in *Following the Equator*. The remark reeks of the self-dislike that was gnawing away at him.

✢ ✢ ✢

Financial disaster would also grow out of triumph. In December 1885, Charles L. Webster and Co. published *The Memoirs of Ulysses S. Grant.* It was a tremendous success, thanks to its readability, the subject matter, and public sympathy for the hard-up family of the great general. Scenting easy profit, Sam ventured further into the business world.

Technology had always fascinated him. He was the first known writer to hand in a typewritten manuscript, and his Hartford house was the first in the city to be fitted with a telephone. Since 1880 he had taken a growing interest in a mechanical typesetting machine invented by James W. Paige. "The Shakespeare of mechanical invention," Sam called him. He was sure the device would earn him a fortune, and in 1886 he increased his backing and agreed to fund all further development. It was a disastrous move.

When it worked, Paige's 18,000-part machine could set type more quickly than six pairs of expert hands. Sadly, it rarely worked. Even when it did, Paige immediately took it to bits to improve it. But the more the machine broke down, the more Sam was sure it needed only a little more time and money to work perfectly. Year by year his investment mounted. In the spring of 1891, hoping to live cheaply in the Old World, he shut down his Hartford home and sailed for Europe with his family. He remained abroad for most of the next nine years.

In 1893 the United States' economy slumped. By the following year, Sam's fortune had been eaten up by lavish living, publishing ventures, and Paige's wretched typesetter. He went into voluntary bankruptcy with debts of over $100,000. For a proud, self-made man, it was the ultimate humiliation. His mood swings became more violent. One day he was the jolly center of the household. The next he shut himself in his room and shouted at anyone who came near him.

✢ ✢ ✢

Sam's finances were rescued by millionaire Henry H. Rogers of Standard Oil. While a heartless monster to competitors, to friends Rogers could be generous and even-handed. Happily, Rogers liked Sam's writing and agreed to help him. He arranged for Livy to own the copyright of Sam's works and drew up a plan for the author to work himself out of debt. Sam insisted he would repay every cent he owed.

His reputation as a writer and speaker had never been higher. In 1895 he started to restore his fortunes by undertaking a hundred-city worldwide lecture tour. It took him from the United States to Australia, New Zealand, India, and South Africa. Huge audiences flocked to hear him, and by January 1898, after three years of nonstop lecturing and writing, he was clear of debt. Four years later, with Rogers still running his finances, he was earning $100,000 a year, with a similar sum in the bank. He was free of financial worries for the rest of his life.

Although living abroad, Sam was now one of the best-known men in America. In 1897, hearing that his obituary had been published, he told the London correspondent of the *New York Journal,* "Reports of my death are greatly exaggerated." When he returned home on October 15, 1900, he was welcomed like a victorious general. He was taken up in a whirl of glamorous, flattering engagements. The constant center of attention, he loved every minute of it. He even said he would run for president—on a platform of being in favor of everything.

✤ ✤ ✤

As Sam's financial worries eased, others rose to take their place. For a number of years Livy had suffered from thyroid heart disease. When she was ill he made himself sick worrying about her. His relationship with her—friend, companion, editor, and lifelong love—had been about the only fixed point in his turbulent life. And she had loyally stuck by him, through all his moods and tantrums. It is no surprise to find his fictional women so much more pleasant than the men.

Sam was also very fond of his daughters, particularly Susy. But they were put off by his unpredictability and short temper. In later life he was shocked to learn that they had always been rather afraid of him. When Susy died of meningitis in August 1896, the news struck him like a physical blow. "It is one of the mysteries of our nature," he said in his *Autobiography*, "that a man,

all unprepared, can receive a thunder-stroke like that and live."

By 1903 Livy was seriously unwell. Sam took her to Florence, where he hoped the air would do her good. He was told to stay away from her room in case he put her under unnecessary strain. The separation was in vain. Olivia Clemens died on June 5, 1904. "She was," Sam mourned, "the most beautiful spirit, and the highest and noblest I have known." Olivia's death became still harder to bear when the depressed Clara entered a sanatorium. Her father was forbidden to visit her for a year.

Public acclaim and inner gloom marked Sam's final years. Honors showered upon him. In 1907 he was awarded an honorary Doctorate of Literature from Oxford University, England. This allowed him to cover his eye-catching white suits with a splendid scarlet gown. He wore the peacock combination whenever it was appropriate—and often when it was not. The university ceremony was followed by a private conversation with Edward VIII, King of England and Emperor of India. The barefoot games beside the Mississippi were but a distant memory.

The following year, Sam moved to Stormfield, an Italian-style villa in Redding, Connecticut. In October 1909 Clara married and moved to Europe with her musician husband. Sam had never known his daughter Jean well, but she now came to live with him and they grew very close. Yet even this friendship was doomed. Jean died of an epileptic seizure on Christmas Eve 1909. Depressed, tired, and without inspiration, Sam declared wretchedly, "I shall never write any more."

That winter his health worsened. He suffered from the sharp chest pains of heart disease—"tobacco heart" he called it—and tried to cut down on his usual forty cigars a day. In the new year he sought comfort in the warmth of Bermuda. It was no use. Drugged with morphine, in April he was brought home to Stormfield where he passed away six days later, aged seventy-five.

Just before he died, Sam Clemens was heard mumbling about the famous split personality of Jekyll and Hyde. Mark Twain's talent for choosing the right phrase had stayed with him to the last.

THE CONTROVERSIAL HISTORY OF
Huckleberry Finn

Two things about *The Adventures of Huckleberry Finn* can be stated with absolute certainty: it is one of the most popular and successful books ever to come out of America, and it is also one of the most controversial. The novel has been criticized on three counts: (1) its language is crude and its tone morally dubious; (2) it promotes a racially prejudiced view of African-Americans; (3) the triumph of the masterly central chapters is spoiled by a weak ending. The third criticism will be discussed in the next chapter.

Nowadays few readers complain that *Huckleberry Finn* is disreputable. In the year of its publication, however, the Library Committee of Concord, Massachusetts, declared it to be "trash and suitable for the slums." Louisa May Alcott, the epitome of respectable, genteel (or, as Huck would say "sivilized") America cried, "If Mr. Clemens cannot think of something better to tell our pure-minded lads and lasses, he had best stop writing for them." Alcott and her kind disliked the book's lack of obvious moral teaching, its pessimism, its satire of aspects of Christian practice, and its use of the language of ordinary people.

The first three objections were a matter of taste, and in time they faded into insignificance. In fact the book's language came to be recognized as its greatest strength. By 1913 H. L. Mencken was calling *Huckleberry Finn* "one of the greatest masterpieces of the world." Ernest Hemingway believed "all modern American literature comes from one book by Mark Twain called *Huckleberry Finn*. . . . It's the best book we've had. All American writing comes from that. There was nothing before. There has been nothing as good since." By the 1920s, most Americans agreed with such sentiments. *Huckleberry Finn* had become an icon of American letters.

In the 1950s, under pressure from the NAACP, an organization devoted to equality for minorities, *Huckleberry Finn* was once again banned from certain public libraries and schoolrooms. This time the charge was not coarseness but racial prejudice. African-Americans were indignant at Clemens's use of the word "nigger." Some felt, too, that the character of Jim, particularly in the closing chapters, was an insulting stereotype.

To counter this, we need to understand straight away that Sam Clemens was no racist. As a child, he often preferred the company of blacks to whites. In adult life he paid for the education of African-Americans, spoke in their churches, and was actively opposed to the often violent racism that still scarred the South. When he spoke of "the reparation due from every white man to every black man," for what had been done in the past, he meant it.

At the same time, Clemens was true to his art. He would not make Jim any less real a human being (and therefore any less real a character) simply because of his racial background. The runaway slave was drawn, just like every other character in the book, with great honesty. Similarly, Clemens put the word "nigger" into Huck's mouth because that was the word a child from his background would have used. It was not an insult. To condemn it as such is either unhelpful prejudice or ignorance.

Finally, modern research suggests a new, broader significance for *Huckleberry Finn*. Critics have always appreciated that Huck speaks a language new to literature. What they have not seen, until recently, is that this language is part black. Consciously or not, the author uses rhythms, syntax, grammar, vocabulary, and irony that owe a good deal to African-American culture. Huck's adventures are in a very real sense multicultural and multi-racial. Perhaps even more than we had previously realized, Sam Clemens is indeed, in the words of Shelley Fisher Fishkin, "the true father of our national heritage."

THE ENDING OF *Huckleberry Finn*

THE FINAL chapters of *Huckleberry Finn* are disappointing. After the wonderfully rich central section of the book describing Jim and Huck's adventures on the Mississippi, particularly those involving the King and the Duke, the ending comes as something of a letdown. The novel seems to lose its tautness, its vitality. Tom's over-elaborate adventure-playing is annoying. It goes on for too long and is not very amusing. Huck and Jim, previously so alive and sympathetic, become lesser people. Huck lets himself be led by the irritating Tom. The serious matter of Jim's freedom is trivialized as he is reduced to a pawn in Tom's silly games. Ernest Hemingway advises readers to stop at the point where Jim is sold back into slavery. "The rest," he said, "is just cheating."

Several scholars have come to the author's defense by suggesting that the concluding section of *Huckleberry Finn* is deliberately disappointing. They point out that by ending the novel as it had begun, with a satire on romantic fiction, Sam gave the work structural symmetry. He also reinforced his central themes—that people are generally unpleasant and that literature deceives. Moreover, it has been suggested that the imprisonment of Jim—his sale back into slavery when in fact he is free—is an allegory on the failure of reconstruction to give African-Americans true liberty.

The trouble with these scholarly defenses of the book's ending is that they are too sophisticated. They unfairly shift criticism from the author to the reader: if readers do not like what they read, argue Clemens's backers, the fault is theirs for not understanding what the author was trying to do. This, of course, is the whining cry of many unsuccessful writers.

Putting "sound heart[s] above deformed conscience[s]," we are all entitled to our opinions about the ending of *Huckleberry Finn*. If we find it long-winded and disappointing, so be it. We are in good company. No novel is perfect. The final chapters of Sam Clemens's finest work may be intellectually sound, but that does not make them artistically successful. It is possible that Clemens himself realized this. After all, why else did he preface the book with the comment "Persons attempting to find a plot . . . will be shot"?

CHRONOLOGY OF THE
LIFE OF SAM CLEMENS/MARK TWAIN

1835	Born in Florida, Missouri.
1839	Family moves to Hannibal, Missouri.
1845	William Owsley shoots Sam Smarr in Hannibal.
1847	Finds body of escaped slave on Sny Island. John Clemens, Sam's father, dies of pneumonia. Sam begins work as an apprentice typesetter.
1849	Works for brother Orion as a typesetter.
1852	First published work, "The Dandy Frightening the Squatter," appears in *The Carpet Bag*.
1853	To St. Louis. Begins work as a traveling printer and editor.
1855	Working for Orion as a printer in Keokuk, Iowa.
1856	Apprenticed to a Mississippi River pilot.
1858	Brother Henry killed.
1859–61	Working as a Mississippi River pilot.
1861	Joins battalion of Confederate irregulars. Deserts and goes to Nevada with brother Orion.
1861–62	Tries (and fails) to make his fortune as a prospector and speculator.
1862	Full-time writer and reporter.
1863	Writes under the name "Mark Twain" for the first time.
1864	Moves to San Francisco.
1865	Achieves nationwide acclaim when the *Saturday Press* of New York publishes "The Celebrated Jumping Frog of Calaveras County."
1866	Writes travel letters from Sandwich Isles (Hawaii). Gives first public lecture.
1867	Sent to New York as a correspondent for the *Alta California*. First book published, incorporating the "Jumping Frog" story. Sails for Europe and the Holy Land as a correspondent on the *Quaker City*. Meets future wife, Olivia Langdon.
1868	First lecture tour.

1869	*The Innocents Abroad* published. Meets lifelong friend and advisor William Dean Howells.
1870	Marries Olivia (Livy) Langdon. Father-in-law dies. Son, Langdon Clemens, born.
1871	Moves to Hartford, Connecticut.
1872	*Roughing It* published. Olivia Susan (Susy) Clemens born. Langdon Clemens dies.
1873	*The Gilded Age,* written with Charles Dudley Warner, published.
1874	Clara Clemens born. Moves to Farmington Avenue, Hartford. *The Gilded Age* becomes a successful stage play.
1876	Begins *Huckleberry Finn. Tom Sawyer* published.
1880	*A Tramp Abroad* published. Jean Clemens born.
1881	*The Prince and the Pauper* published.
1882	Visit to the Mississippi.
1883	*Huckleberry Finn* finished. *Life on the Mississippi* published.
1884	Charles L. Webster Publishing Co. established. *Huckleberry Finn* published in Britain.

1885   Begins dictating his *Autobiography*, which he continues, on and
        off, for the rest of his life, but nothing appears in print until after
        his death. *Huckleberry Finn* published in U.S.A. Charles L. Webster
        publishes *The Memoirs of Ulysses S. Grant.*
1886   Heavy investment in Paige Typesetter.
1889   *A Connecticut Yankee in King Arthur's Court* published. Further
        investment in Paige Typesetter.
1891   Clemens family moves to Europe for almost nine years.
1894   Declared bankrupt. Henry H. Rogers becomes financial advisor.
        Pudd'nhead Wilson published.
1895   Worldwide lecture tour to pay debts.
1896   Susy Clemens dies.
1897   *Following the Equator* published.
1898   Clear of debt.
1900   Returns to hero's welcome in U.S.A.
1904   Olivia Clemens dies.
1907   Honorary doctorate from Oxford University.
1909   Clara Clemens marries. Jean Clemens comes to live with her father.
        Jean dies.
1910   Sam Clemens dies.

FURTHER READING

Among the many editions of *Huckleberry Finn*, students may find these the most useful:

Bradley, Scully, Richmond Croom Beatty, E. Hudson Long, and Thomas Cooley, eds. *The Adventures of Huckleberry Finn*, 2d ed. New York: Norton Critical Edition, 1977.

Coveney, Peter, ed. *The Adventures of Huckleberry Finn*. New York: Penguin Classics, 1985

CONTEMPORARY WORKS ABOUT TWAIN:

Clemens, Susy. *Papa, an Intimate Biography of Mark Twain by His Daughter Susy Clemens, Thirteen; With a Foreword and Copious Comments by Her Father*. Edited by Charles Neider. Garden City, N.Y: Doubleday, 1985.

Howells, William Dean. *My Mark Twain: Reminiscences and Criticisms*. New York: Harper and Brothers, 1910.

Neider, Charles, ed. *The Autobiography of Mark Twain*. New York: Harper & Row, 1959.

Paine, Albert Bigelow, ed. *Mark Twain's Letters*. New York: Harper, 1917. Reprint, New York: AMS Press Inc., 1975.

SECONDARY SOURCES:

Doyno, Victor. *Writing Huck Finn: Mark Twain's Creative Process*. Philadelphia: University of Pennsylvania Press, 1991.

Fishkin, Shelley Fisher. *Was Huck Black? Mark Twain and African-American Voices*. New York: Oxford University Press, 1993.

Kaplan, Justin. *Mr. Clemens and Mark Twain*. New York: Simon and Schuster, 1966.

Paine, Albert Bigelow. *Mark Twain*. New York: Harper, 1912. Reprint, n.p.: Reprint Services Corporation, 1992.

Wecter, Dixon. *Sam Clemens of Hannibal*. Boston: Houghton Mifflin, 1952. Reprint, New York: AMS Press Inc., 1977.

Stewart Ross has taught history and English in England, Saudi Arabia, and America. He is now a full-time writer. Among his many works for young readers are *Charlotte Brontë and Jane Eyre* and *Shakespeare and Macbeth*, an ALA Best Book for Young Adults. He lives in Canterbury, England.

Ronald Himler studied painting and illustration at the Cleveland Institute of Art and the Cranbrook Academy of Art. He has illustrated more than seventy-five books for children, including Eve Bunting's *The Wall* and Ellen Howard's *The Log Cabin Quilt*, winner of the Christopher Award.

A painter of Plains Indian culture for galleries in the Southwest, Mr. Himler lives in Tucson, Arizona.